Safeguarding and children, young people or vulnerable adults

Subject	Section	Page
Contents		1
Introduction to safeguarding	01	02
Safeguarding legislation and guidance	02	05
Indicators of abuse or neglect	03	15
Making judgements	04	37
Communicating worries and concerns	05	42
Roles and responsibilities	06	45
Sharing information	07	54
Allegations and complaints	08	59
Reporting allegations and complaints in the workplace	09	63
Useful reference links	10	80

Safeguarding and Protecting Children, Young People or Vulnerable Adults is published by: **Nuco Training Ltd**

Safeguarding is a term we use to describe how we protect children and vulnerable adults from abuse or neglect. It is an important shared priority of many public services and a key responsibility of local authorities.

Setting up and following good safeguarding policies and procedures means children and vulnerable adults can be safe from other adults and children who might pose a risk.

Safeguarding children and young people includes:

- Protecting children from maltreatment
- Preventing impairment of children's health or development
- Ensuring that children grow up in circumstances consistent with the provision of safe and effective care
- Taking action to enable all children to have the best outcomes

Safeguarding vulnerable adults includes:

- Protecting their rights to live in safety, free from abuse and neglect
- People and organisations working together to prevent the risk of abuse or neglect and to stop them from happening
- Making sure people's wellbeing is promoted, taking their views, wishes, feelings and beliefs into account

DEFINITION OF A CHILD

Anyone who has not yet reached their 18th birthday. 'Children' therefore, means 'children and young people' throughout this publication.

The very young, disabled and isolated are particularly vulnerable due to many factors, including:

- Levels of dependence
- Inability to resist or avoid
- Communication issues

DEFINITION OF A VULNERABLE ADULT ('ADULT AT RISK')

An adult at risk is any person who is aged 18 years or over and at risk of abuse or neglect because of their needs for care and/or support. Where someone is over 18 but is still receiving children's services and a safeguarding issue is raised, the matter should be dealt with as a matter of course by the adult safeguarding team.

There is a danger that some adults at risk do not easily fit into this definition and may be overlooked.

Examples of people in vulnerable circumstances might be:

- Adults with low level mental health problems
- Adults with low level learning disabilities
- Older people living independently within the community
- Adults with substance misuse problems
- Adults self-directing their care

WHAT IS CHILD PROTECTION?

A process for responding to individual children who are suffering or likely to suffer, significant harm as a result of abuse or neglect.

Child protection is part of safeguarding and refers to activities undertaken to prevent children suffering, or likely to suffer, significant harm.

SAFEGUARDING ASSESSMENT FRAMEWORK

The Assessment Framework can be represented in the form of a triangle, with the child's welfare at the centre. This highlights that all assessment activity and subsequent planning and provision of services must focus on ensuring that the child's welfare is safeguarded and promoted.

A good assessment is one which investigates all three areas, represented on each side of the triangle:

- **The child's developmental needs, including whether they are suffering, or likely to suffer, significant harm**
- **Parents' or carers' capacity to respond to those needs**
- **The impact and influence of wider family, community and environmental circumstances**

ASSESSMENT FRAMEWORK

ASSESSMENT FRAMEWORK

CHILD'S DEVELOPMENT NEEDS
- Health
- Education
- Emotional & Behaviourial Development
- Identity
- Family & Social Relationships
- Social Presentation
- Selfcare Skills

PARENTING CAPACITY
- Basic Care
- Ensuring Safety
- Emotional Warmth
- Stimulation
- Guidance & Boundaries
- Stability

CHILD SAFEGUARDING AND PROMOTING WELFARE

FAMILY & ENVIRONMENTAL FACTORS
- Community Resources
- Family Social Integration
- Income
- Employment
- Housing
- Wider Family
- Family History & Functioning

Legislation has been applied to safeguard and protect children, young people and vulnerable adults in the UK.

England, Northern Ireland, Scotland and Wales each have their own framework, setting out the duties and responsibilities of organisations to keep children and vulnerable adults safe.

CHILDREN ACT 1989

The Children Act 1989 is seen as the first significant law which put in place most of the child protection structures and principles we use today.

The Act allocates duties to all parties involved, including local authorities, the police, parents and other agencies in the United Kingdom, to ensure children are safeguarded and their welfare is promoted.

It centres on the idea that children are best cared for within their own families; however, it also makes provisions for instances when parents and families do not co-operate with statutory bodies.

THE VICTORIA CLIMBIÉ INQUIRY

Over the past two decades, there have been many child abuse cases that have prompted a series of overhauls to child protection procedures. One of the most significant cases being the tragic death of Victoria Climbié in February 2000.

Victoria suffered unimaginable injuries after months of abuse from her Great Aunt Marie-Thérèse Kouao and her boyfriend Carl Manning.

Victoria died on the 25th February 2000 with 128 separate injuries to her body.

Despite Victoria coming into contact with the police, local authorities, social care services and visiting the hospital twice after sustaining severe injuries, the abuse and neglect did not come to light until after her death.

Almost a year after Victoria's death, Carl Manning and Marie-Thérèse Kouao were found guilty of murder, although both denied the charges.

A significant statement was made during the trial and that is that the blame lay not only with Kouao and Manning, but with the Child Protection Authorities who had been 'blindingly incompetent'.

Due to the severity of Victoria's case, the government announced a public inquiry into the death, headed by Lord Laming. This was the first inquiry in Britain to use a wide range of powers to look into everything from the role of social care services to police child protection measures.

Lord Laming was instructed to make recommendations on how the system should change, to ensure cases like this do not happen again.

The Victoria Climbié Inquiry:
Report of an inquiry by Lord
Laming 28th January 2003

EVERY CHILD MATTERS

'Every child matters' is a green paper published by the UK labour government in 2003. This document outlines the government's proposals for the reform and improvement of child care, following the death of Victoria Climbié and subsequent investigations by Lord Laming.

The document applies to children and young people from when they are born, up until they reach the age of 19.

The policy is based on the idea that every child, regardless of their individual circumstances or background, should be given the utmost of support throughout their lives.

There are 5 key outcomes that children, young people and their families requested during consultation with the UK labour government.

These are:

- **To be healthy**
- **To stay safe**
- **To enjoy and achieve**
- **To make a positive contribution**
- **To achieve economic well-being**

The policy applies to everyone who works with children, or provides services to children. This includes professionals such as teachers, hospital staff, foster carers, social care services and the police.

The idea is that at the core of all the work they do, these five key outcomes should be remembered and implemented, to ensure children get the best start in life.

WORKING TOGETHER TO SAFEGUARD CHILDREN (2018)

A guide to inter-agency working to safeguard and promote the welfare of children.

This is the key statutory guidance for anyone who works with children in England. It sets out how organisations and individuals should work together and how practitioners should conduct assessments for children.

This guidance document has a robust focus on putting children at the centre of the safeguarding system and encourages every individual and agency to play their full part, working together to meet the needs of the most vulnerable of children.

WHAT TO DO IF YOU'RE WORRIED A CHILD IS BEING ABUSED (2015)

This non-statutory guidance document was produced to help practitioners identify abuse and neglect and take appropriate action in response. It draws on both 'Working Together to Safeguard Children' and the 'Assessment Framework' in a format which is manageable and accessible for practitioners.

KEEPING CHILDREN SAFE IN EDUCATION (2021)

This is statutory guidance from the Department for Education.

Schools and colleges must refer to it when carrying out their duties to safeguard and promote the welfare of children within their remit.

THE UNITED NATIONS CONVENTION ON THE RIGHTS OF THE CHILD 1989

This convention sets out the international agreement on minimum standards for protecting children's rights, including:

- Life, survival and development
- Protection from violence, abuse or neglect
- An education that enables children to fulfil their potential
- Be raised by, or have a relationship with, their parents
- Express their opinions and be listened to

THE CARE ACT 2014

The Care Act is the most significant reform of social care in over 60 years, replacing most previous law relating to carers and vulnerable adults being cared for. The Act aims to clarify the duties of local authorities and other bodies and to ensure vulnerable people are aware of what care and support they are entitled to.

*The Care Act enshrines the following principles, which underpin all adult safeguarding work:

- **Empowerment** - presumption of person led decisions and informed consent
- **Prevention** - it is better to take action before harm occurs
- **Proportionality** - proportionate and least intrusive response appropriate to the risk presented
- **Protection** - support and representation for those in greatest need
- **Partnership** - local solutions through services working with their communities. Communities have a part to play in preventing, detecting and reporting neglect and abuse
- **Accountability** - Accountability and transparency in delivering safeguarding

Agencies can use the principles to benchmark existing adult safeguarding arrangements to see how far they support this aim and to measure future improvements.

*HM Government, Adult Safeguarding:
Statement of Government Policy on Adult Safeguarding Department of Health, 2013
Web link: www.gov.uk/government/publications/adult-safeguarding-statement-of-government-policy-10-may-2013

SAFEGUARDING VULNERABLE GROUPS ACT 2006

This Act of Parliament was created to help avoid harm, or risk of harm, by preventing people who are deemed unsuitable to work with children or vulnerable adults from gaining access to them through their work.

The Act places a statutory duty on all those working with vulnerable groups to register and undergo an advanced vetting process with criminal sanctions for non-compliance.

The Independent Safeguarding Authority was set-up by the UK government as a result of the Safeguarding Vulnerable Groups Act 2006, in order to assess the suitability of anyone who wants to work with children or vulnerable adults.

The Independent Safeguarding Authority worked in conjunction with the Criminal Records Bureau (CRB) to protect vulnerable groups by checking anyone they may come into contact with during employment situations.

DISCLOSURE AND BARRING SERVICE (DBS)

On the 1st December 2012, the Independent Safeguarding Authority merged with the Criminal Records Bureau (CRB) to become the Disclosure and Barring Service (DBS) which we know today.

A DBS (Disclosure and Barring Service) check is a record of an individual's unprotected convictions, cautions, reprimands and warnings and can also include intelligence held by the police.

The DBS enables organisations in the public, private and voluntary sectors to make safer recruitment decisions by identifying candidates who may be unsuitable for certain work, especially that involve children or vulnerable adults.

THE MENTAL CAPACITY ACT 2005

Designed to protect and empower individuals who may lack the mental capacity to make their own decisions about their care and treatment. It is a law that applies to individuals aged 16 and over.

Other examples of people who may lack capacity include those with:

- Dementia
- A severe learning disability
- A brain injury
- A mental health condition
- A stroke
- Unconsciousness caused by an anaesthetic or sudden accident

However, just because a person has one of these conditions it does not necessarily mean they lack the capacity to make a specific decision.

Someone can lack capacity to make some decisions but still have the capacity to make other decisions (for example, to decide what items to buy at the local shop).

LEGISLATION RELATING TO VULNERABLE ADULTS EXPLAINED

Whilst there are many specific pieces of legislation and guidance documents which have been implemented over the years to safeguard and protect children and young people in the UK, only Scotland at present has legislation specifically relating to safeguarding and the protection of vulnerable adults.

However, this does not mean that there are no powers to act. There is a wide range of other legislation currently in force throughout the UK which is very relevant and applicable to adults whom may be at risk and it is important you are aware of this and how it may be used.

In addition to specific safeguarding legislation and guidance, other regulatory requirements, such as government standards, occupational standards, professional standards, codes of conduct and inspection frameworks should also be considered.

Legislation, regulatory requirements and statutory guidance places particular responsibilities and duties onto organisations and individuals that work directly with, and whose work affects children and vulnerable adults.

THE RIGHTS OF AN ADULT AT RISK

The Human Rights Act 1998 provides all citizens with basic human rights, including:

- **Your right to life**
- **Your right to not be tortured or be treated in an inhuman way**
- **Your right to family life**

The Act also places a duty on public bodies to intervene proportionately to protect these rights for all.

OTHER LEGISLATION THAT COULD BE RELEVANT

It must be emphasised that this list is by no means definitive:

- Adoption and Children Act 2002
- Care Standards Act 2000
- Childcare Act 2006
- Children and Young Persons Act 2008
- Children and Families Act 2014
- Common Law Duty of Care
- Counter-Terrorism and Security Act 2015
- Domestic Violence Crime and Victims Act 2004
- Education Act 2011
- Equality Act 2010
- Female Genital Mutilation Act 2003
- Health and Social Care Act 2012
- Human Rights Act 1998
- Mental Health Act 2007
- NHS & Community Care Act 1990
- Protection of Freedoms Act 2012
- Sexual Offences Act 2003

WHAT IS SIGNIFICANT HARM?

The term 'significant harm' can include any form of abuse, neglect, accident or injury that is sufficiently serious to adversely affect progress and enjoyment of someone's life.

Harm is defined as the ill-treatment or impairment of health and development.

As there is no absolute criteria for identifying significant harm, it will prove useful to consider the following factors:

- **The nature, degree and extent of physical harm**
- **The duration and frequency of abuse or neglect**
- **The extent of premeditation**
- **The degree of threats and intimidation**
- **Evidence of aggression and bizarre or unusual elements in child/adult sexual abuse**

WHAT IS ABUSE?

Abuse is the violation of an individual's human and civil rights by any other person or persons. The abuse can vary from treating someone with disrespect in a way which significantly affects the person's quality of life, to causing actual physical suffering.

WHAT IS NEGLECT?

Neglect is the persistent failure to meet a person's basic physical and/or psychological needs, likely to result in the serious impairment of a person's health or development.

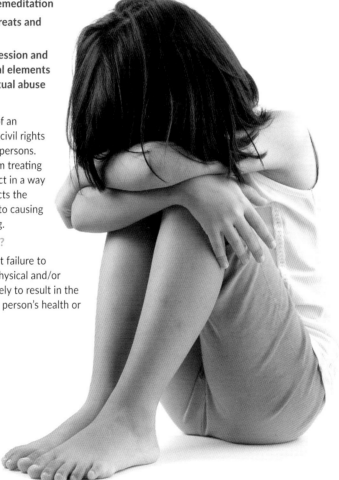

FORMS AND CHARACTERISTICS OF ABUSE

Although it is very difficult to accept, child and adult abuse does happen and is unfortunately an all too common occurrence across most cultures and countries. Any child or adult, regardless of their age, gender, race, religion, culture or social background may be at risk of physical, sexual or psychological harm and a potential victim of abuse.

There is, however, evidence to suggest that incidents of abuse can be reduced and often prevented through implementation of national strategies aimed at promoting human rights and reducing the risks of child and adult abuse occurring.

The different types of abuse can fall into the following categories:

- Physical abuse
- Domestic abuse
- Sexual abuse
- Modern slavery
- Self-neglect
- Emotional or psychological abuse
- Financial or material abuse
- Discriminatory abuse
- Organisational or institutional abuse
- Neglect or acts of omission

PHYSICAL ABUSE

This may involve hitting, shaking, slapping, pushing, kicking, poisoning, drowning, burning, scalding, restraint or restricting someone from doing things at certain times.

Children can get cuts and bruises during their everyday life and this can be part of their normal development.

For example:

- A toddler learning to walk may tumble and bump their head
- An infant running may trip and graze their knee
- A child learning to ride their bike might catch their ankles on the frame or fall off and bruise their elbow
- A teenager might fall off their skateboard and fracture their arm
- An adult may trip and fall or injure themselves during their day to day activities

The above examples can make it difficult to ascertain if a child or vulnerable adult is being physically abused. When injuries have occurred it's always important to listen to what the child or adult tells you, if they are able to.

You need to consider if their story matches with the nature of the injuries and all other available information before reaching a conclusion.

Certain locations on the body are more likely to sustain accidental injury. These include the knees, elbows, shins and forehead.

Protected body parts and soft tissue areas such as the back, thighs, genital area, buttocks, back of the legs or face are less likely to accidentally come into contact with objects that could cause injury.

INDICATORS OF PHYSICAL ABUSE

- Injuries in unusual positions which it's hard to explain the nature of i.e. back, chest, torso, buttocks, neck, behind ears, inside thighs, face, head, genitals or back of the hand

- Injuries inconsistent with the age, abilities or lifestyle of the child

- Apparent finger marks, slap marks, bites, fractures, burns and scalds

- Damage to the mouth such as bruised or cut lips or torn skin where the upper lip joins the mouth

- Clusters of injuries forming regular patterns

- Injuries at different stages of healing

- Object marks and clear outlines of objects

- The child appears frightened

- An explanation of injuries is avoided or inconsistent

- Delay in seeking treatment for injuries

- The child behaving aggressively towards others

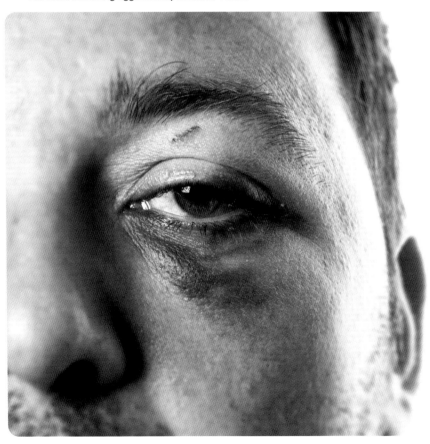

DOMESTIC ABUSE

This may include physical, sexual, psychological or emotional abuse between those aged 16 or over who are, or have been intimate partners or family members regardless of gender or sexuality.

Exposure to domestic abuse can include seeing or hearing the ill-treatment of others.

Frequent and/or prolonged exposure can have a serious impact on a child's development, emotional well-being and can also have an impact on their education.

SEXUAL ABUSE

Sexual abuse involves forcing or enticing a child, young person or vulnerable adult to take part in sexual activities, not necessarily involving a high level of violence, whether or not the individual is aware of what is happening.

The activities may involve physical contact, including assault by penetration (for example, rape or oral sex) or non-penetrative acts such as masturbation, kissing, rubbing and touching outside of clothing.

They may also include non-contact activities, such as involving children or adults in looking at, or in the production of sexual images, watching sexual activities, encouraging children to behave in sexually inappropriate ways, or grooming a child or vulnerable adult in preparation for abuse.

Sexual abuse is not solely perpetrated by adult males. Women can also commit acts of sexual abuse, as can other children.

Indicators of sexual abuse

- A detailed sexual knowledge inappropriate to the age and developmental stage of the child
- Sexually explicit language and behaviour
- Increased frequency of visits to the toilet or bed wetting
- Behaviour that is excessively affectionate or sexual towards other children or adults
- A fear of medical examinations
- A fear of being alone
- Sudden loss of appetite, compulsive eating, anorexia nervosa or bulimia nervosa
- Excessive masturbation
- Concerning behaviours by adults, for example, grooming or unusual interest in a specific child
- Unexplained gifts or new possessions
- Children who go missing from home or education
- Changes in mood or sudden withdrawal from activities

BROOK TRAFFIC LIGHT TOOL

The Brook Traffic Light Tool is a useful resource for professionals to use to assess whether the sexual behaviour of a child is appropriate for the age of that child. It may be used to assist you to identify, assess and respond appropriately to sexual behaviours.

EMOTIONAL ABUSE

Emotional abuse is the persistent emotional maltreatment of a child or adult such as to cause severe and persistent adverse effects on the child's or adult's mental health and self-esteem.

Indicators of emotional abuse

- Physical, mental and emotional developmental delays
- Difficulty with genuine trust, intimacy and affection
- Negative, hopeless and negative view of self, family and society
- Lack of empathy, compassion and remorse
- Low self-esteem, deference and resignation
- Change in appetite
- Extremes of passivity and aggression
- Poor concentration
- Difficulty making friends
- Sudden speech disorders
- Unexplained fear and/or defensiveness
- Emotional withdrawal
- Sleep disturbance
- Carer constantly rejects and ignores the child, depriving them of responsiveness and stimulation
- Carer isolates the child and prevents them building relationships and making friends
- Carer shows little warmth and affection towards the child
- Carer constantly criticises or humiliates the child and appears unable to give praise

FINANCIAL OR MATERIAL ABUSE

This may involve theft, fraud, exploitation, pressure in connection with wills, property or inheritance, financial transactions or the misuse or misappropriation of property, possessions or benefits.

Indicators of financial or material abuse

- Unexplained sudden inability to pay bills or maintain lifestyle
- Unusual or inappropriate bank account activity
- Withholding money
- Recent change of deeds or title of property
- Unusual interest shown by family or other in the individual's assets
- Person managing financial affairs is evasive or uncooperative
- Misappropriation of benefits and/or use of the individual's money by other members of the household
- Fraud or intimidation in connection with wills, property or other assets

MODERN SLAVERY

This encompasses slavery, human trafficking, forced labour and domestic servitude.

Traffickers and slave masters use whatever means they have at their disposal to coerce, deceive and force individuals into a life of abuse, servitude and inhumane treatment.

Indicators of modern slavery

- Poor dishevelled appearance
- Poor command of English or awareness of local environment
- Unwillingness to provide basic information about self

DISCRIMINATORY ABUSE

This may involve types of harassment or insults because of someone's race, gender, gender identity, age, disability, sexual orientation or religion.

Indicators of discriminatory abuse

- **Lack of respect shown to an individual**
- **Signs of a sub-standard service offered to an individual**
- **Repeated exclusion from rights afforded to citizens such as health, education, employment, criminal justice and civic status**

ORGANISATIONAL ABUSE

This may include neglect and poor care in an institution or care setting such as a hospital or care home, or if an organisation provides care in someone's home.

Indicators of organisational abuse

- **Repeated failures on the part of an organisation, despite warnings and agreement to improve**
- **Routine acceptance of poor practice**

Workers across a wide range of organisations need to be vigilant about adult safeguarding concerns in all walks of life including health and social care, welfare, policing, banking, fire and rescue services, trading standards, leisure services, faith groups and housing.

GP's in particular are often well-placed to notice changes in an adult that may indicate they are being abused or neglected.

Findings from serious case reviews have sometimes stated that if professionals or other staff had acted upon their concerns or sought more information, then death or serious harm might have been prevented.

NEGLECT OR ACTS OF OMISSION

This may include ignoring medical or physical care needs, failure to provide access to appropriate health, social care or educational services, the withholding of the necessities of life, such as medication, adequate nutrition and heating.

Long term, sustained neglect is damaging emotionally, socially and educationally and is likely to cause far more developmental delays and medical impairments than any other form of abuse.

Indicators of neglect and acts of omission

- **Failure to thrive**
- **Constant hunger and/or tiredness, malnutrition, steals food**
- **Poor hygiene**
- **Frequent accidental injuries and illnesses**
- **Untreated medical problems**
- **Developmental delays**
- **Poor state of clothing**
- **Unable to make friends, lack of social relationships**
- **Low self esteem**
- **Treated differently to other children by their carer**
- **Carer appears stressed and unable to cope**

SELF-NEGLECT

Self-neglect covers a wide range of behaviour neglecting to care for one's personal hygiene, health or surroundings.

The definition of self-neglect excludes a situation in which a mentally competent older person, who understands the consequences of their decisions, makes a conscious and voluntary decision to engage in acts that threaten their health or safety as a matter of personal choice.

Indicators of self-neglect

- **Very poor personal hygiene**
- **Lack of essential food, clothing or shelter**
- **Malnutrition and/or dehydration**
- **Neglecting household maintenance**
- **Collecting a large number of animals in inappropriate conditions**
- **Non-compliance with health or care services**
- **Inability or unwillingness to take medication or treat illness or injury**

ADULTS LIVING IN VULNERABLE CIRCUMSTANCES

Adults living in vulnerable circumstances are often over-looked in the context of safeguarding.

This can include:

- **Older people living independently within the community who have inadequate or no support**
- **Adults with cognitive impairment or no form of verbal communication**
- **Homelessness or living in squalid/unsafe conditions**
- **Adults whose physical disability or chronic illness, including addiction, does not allow them to adequately care for themselves**
- **Adults whose care needs are not being adequately met by their carer or care organisation**
- **Adults with capacity, who are not given voice or choice in their care or whose choices disregarded without adequate purpose**

FORCED MARRIAGE

Forced marriage takes place when the bride, groom or both do not want to get married but are forced to do so by others.

People forced into marriage may be tricked into going abroad, physically threatened and/or emotionally blackmailed to do so. Unlike arranged marriages where the bride and groom have the choice whether they want to marry, there is no freedom of choice in a forced marriage.

It can affect men, women, boy and girls; it is unacceptable and cannot be justified on any religious or cultural basis.

COUNTY LINE GANGS

County lines is a term used to describe gangs and organised criminal networks involved in exporting illegal drugs into one or more importing areas within the UK, using dedicated mobile phone lines or other form of "deal line".

They are likely to exploit children and adults at risk to move and store the drugs and money, and they will often use coercion, intimidation, violence (including sexual violence) and weapons.

HATE CRIME

Hate crimes are discriminatory acts towards an individual motivated by another's hostility, prejudice or hatred based upon who or what they believe or perceive the other to be.

This may involve an individual being targeted because of their race, religion or belief, sexual orientation, transgender or disability.

These incidents can involve verbal or physical abuse, threatening behaviour or actual violence.

Such incidents may also result in an individual being discriminated against under the Equality Act 2010.

MATE CRIME

Mate Crime is a form of crime in which a perpetrator befriends a vulnerable person with the intention of then exploiting the person financially, physically or sexually.

Victims of mate crime may be enticed into committing criminal acts themselves and taking the blame to protect the real perpetrator.

BULLYING

Bullying is also recognised as a type of abuse. It is always distressing for the victim and can have serious consequences. Therefore, it should always be taken seriously.

It occurs when an individual or group of individuals show hostility towards another individual. It can include physical abuse such as hitting or pushing and verbal abuse including name-calling and spreading rumours.

Bullying can happen at school, at home, in the workplace or in the community. It can hurt both children and adults physically and emotionally.

ELECTRONIC MEDIA ABUSE

The internet can be used as a media to abuse children or adults at risk. Common ways in which a person can be abused through the internet include:

- **Circulation of pictures and videos of abuse**
- **A person being groomed for the purposes of abuse**
- **Exposure to sexual and other offensive content**
- **The use of the internet to engage a person in extremist ideologies**

Indicators that a child or adult at risk is being abused through the internet can include:

- **Changes in behaviour and mood**
- **Inappropriate images, videos or chat logs being found on an electronic device**
- **A person being overly protective or secretive of an electronic device**
- **Changes to the person's circle of friends**
- **Not wanting to be alone, or in the company of, a certain person**

FEMALE GENITAL MUTILATION (FGM)

Female genital mutilation (FGM) is also known as "female circumcision" or "cutting".

It is a procedure where the female genitals are deliberately cut, injured or changed, but where there's no medical reason for this to be done. This procedure is illegal in the UK and is a form of child abuse.

As from October 2015 there is a mandatory reporting duty placed upon teachers, social care workers and healthcare professionals to report to the police where they discover that FGM appears to have been carried out on a girl under 18.

TERRORISM, EXTREMISM AND RADICALISATION

Terrorism and extremism in the UK can involve the exploitation of vulnerable people including adults and children. This can include involving them in extremist activity in the UK and overseas.

Individuals involved in extremist activity come from a range of backgrounds and experiences - there is no such thing as a "typical extremist".

They can be male or female, rich or poor, young or old. They believe that violence is an acceptable method of changing how others think and behave.

People may become involved in terrorism or violent extremism for many reasons, including:

- **To defend their culture and beliefs**
- **Peer pressure by friends or family**
- **A lack of identity in society**
- **Radicalised by extremist groups**
- **They may be seeking vengeance or retaliation**

Extremists who encourage and motivate individuals to commit crime and acts of violent extremism often target individuals who are vulnerable. These individuals are led to believe that the activities they are taking part in will earn them respect, acceptance, wealth and riches.

TERRORISM *

Terrorism is defined as an action that; endangers or causes serious violence to a person or people, causing serious damage to property or seriously interferes or disrupts an electronic system.

The use of threat must be designed to influence the government or to intimidate the public and is made for the purpose of political, religious or ideological gain.

> *
> Terrorism Act 2000

EXTREMISM **

Extremism is vocal or active opposition to fundamental British values, including democracy, the rule of law, individual liberty and mutual respect and tolerance of different faiths and beliefs.

> **
> HM Government Prevent Strategy 2011

RADICALISATION ***

Radicalisation refers to the process by which a person comes to support terrorism and forms of extremism leading to terrorism.

> ***
> HM Government Prevent Strategy 2011

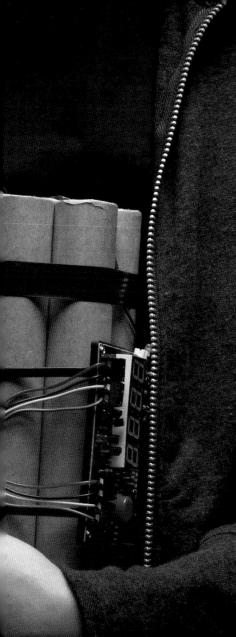

PREVENT STRATEGY ****

'Prevent' is the national government strategy to respond to the challenge of extremism and prevent people from being drawn into terrorism. It is part of a broader counter terrorism strategy known as 'Contest'. The aim of the Prevent strategy is to stop people becoming terrorists or supporting terrorism.

The strategy sets three objectives:

Ideology:

Challenging the ideology that supports terrorism and those who promote it

Individuals:

Protecting people being drawn into terrorism and ensure that they are given appropriate advice and support

Institutions:

Supporting sectors and institutions where there are risks of radicalisation

****
HM Government Prevent Strategy 2011

CHANNEL *****

'Channel' is a key element of the Prevent strategy and is a multi-agency approach to protect people at risk from radicalisation. Channel is about safeguarding children, young people and adults from being drawn into committing terrorist related activity. It is about early identification, intervention and prevention to protect and divert people away from the risk they face before illegality occurs.

*****
HM Government Channel Duty Guidance 2012

INDICATORS OF VULNERABILITY TO RADICALISATION CAN INCLUDE:

Identity crisis – the individual is distanced from their religious and cultural heritage.

Personal crisis – the individual may have detached from their existing friendship group and become involved with a new group of friends. They may be seeking answers to questions relating to their identity, beliefs and belonging in society.

Personal circumstances – migration, community tensions and events affecting the individual's country or region of origin.

Unmet aspirations – perceptions of injustice, a feeling of failure and rejection of civic life

Experiences of criminality – involvement with criminal groups, imprisonment and poor resettlement and reintegration.

Special educational need – individuals experiencing difficulties with social interaction, difficulty empathising with others and understanding the consequences of their actions.

MORE CRITICAL RISK INDICATORS COULD INCLUDE:

- Joining or seeking to join extremist organisations
- Becoming more argumentative over their view points, condemning those who disagree and ignoring opinions that contradict their own
- Being overly secretive about what they are accessing and viewing online
- Downloading extremist literature and promoting its content
- Using extremist narratives and a global ideology to explain personal disadvantage
- Losing interest in activities they used to enjoy, distancing themselves from friends and family
- Experiencing a high level of social isolation
- Altering their style of clothing and personal appearance
- Irregular travel patterns and frequent overseas visits
- Justifying the use of violence to solve societal issues

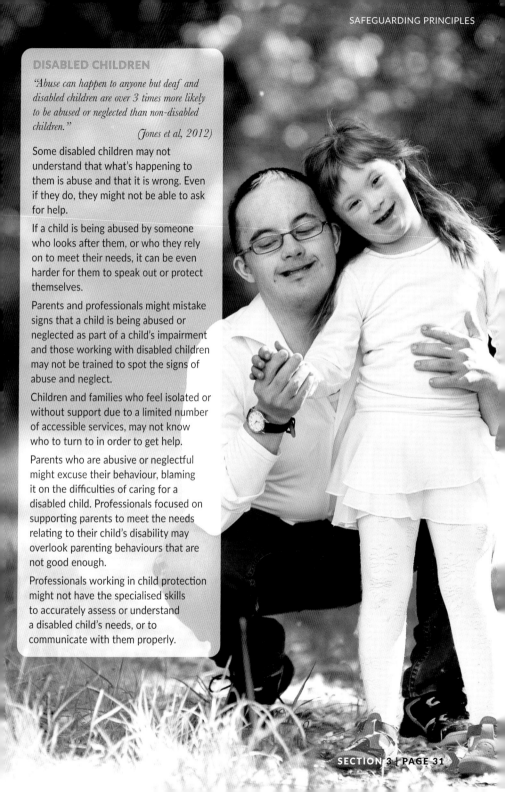

DISABLED CHILDREN

"Abuse can happen to anyone but deaf and disabled children are over 3 times more likely to be abused or neglected than non-disabled children."

(Jones et al, 2012)

Some disabled children may not understand that what's happening to them is abuse and that it is wrong. Even if they do, they might not be able to ask for help.

If a child is being abused by someone who looks after them, or who they rely on to meet their needs, it can be even harder for them to speak out or protect themselves.

Parents and professionals might mistake signs that a child is being abused or neglected as part of a child's impairment and those working with disabled children may not be trained to spot the signs of abuse and neglect.

Children and families who feel isolated or without support due to a limited number of accessible services, may not know who to turn to in order to get help.

Parents who are abusive or neglectful might excuse their behaviour, blaming it on the difficulties of caring for a disabled child. Professionals focused on supporting parents to meet the needs relating to their child's disability may overlook parenting behaviours that are not good enough.

Professionals working in child protection might not have the specialised skills to accurately assess or understand a disabled child's needs, or to communicate with them properly.

CHILDREN IN CARE

Most children who are in care live safely but a small number do experience harm. There are several risk factors related to being in care which can make children more vulnerable to abuse and neglect.

CHILDREN WHO HAVE EXPERIENCED OTHER FORMS OF ABUSE

Children who have been abused or neglected in the past are more likely to experience further abuse than children who haven't been abused or neglected. This is known as revictimisation.

Children who are being abused or neglected are also likely to be experiencing another form of abuse at the same time. This is known as polyvictimisation.

CHILDREN FROM BLACK AND MIXED ETHNIC BACKGROUNDS

There doesn't appear to be links between ethnic groups and child abuse or neglect, but children from black and mixed ethnic backgrounds are over-represented in the care system and in the 'children in need' statistics.

This may be a result of a variety of issues, including:

- Racial discrimination
- Language barriers
- Community and cultural norms and practices, such as female genital mutilation or harsh physical discipline
- Inadequate or inappropriate services
- No action being taken for fear of upsetting cultural norms

THE VULNERABILITY OF BABIES *

All Babies Count: Prevention and protection for vulnerable babies

This NSPCC report includes analysis into the number of babies under 1 year who are affected by parental substance misuse, mental illness and domestic abuse which are all important risk factors for abuse and neglect.

Babies are almost entirely dependent on their immediate caregivers. A parent's capacity to respond appropriately to the emotions and needs of their babies has a profound impact.

Becoming a new parent is a major transition; there are times when every parent feels under pressure and may struggle to cope with the stresses and responsibilities of their role. But, for very young parents, or parents facing additional challenges in their lives such as mental illness and domestic abuse, this can be a particularly difficult time.

All babies need to be safe, nurtured and able to thrive. The early care they receive provides the essential foundations for all future physical, social and emotional development. Whilst most parents do provide the love and care their babies need, sadly too many babies suffer abuse and neglect.

*
All Babies Count: Prevention and protection for vulnerable babies
Credit: NSPCC report by Chris Cuthbert, Gwynne Rayns and Kate Stanley (2011)

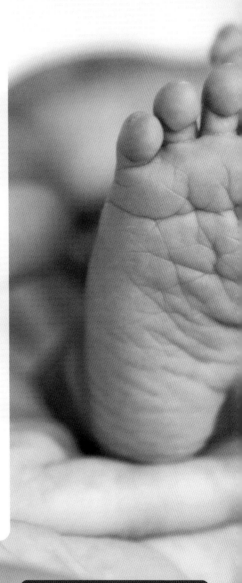

THE VULNERABILITY OF BABIES - STATISTICS *

The emotional abuse, neglect or physical harm of babies is particularly shocking both because babies are totally dependent on others and because of the relative prevalence of such maltreatment:

- **45% of serious case reviews in England relate to babies under the age of 1 year**
- **In England and Wales, babies are eight times more likely to be killed than older children**

Original analysis conducted estimates for the first time the numbers of babies living in vulnerable and complex family situations.

In the UK, an estimated:

- **19,500 babies under 1 year old are living with a parent who has used Class A drugs in the last year**
- **39,000 babies under 1 year old live in households affected by domestic violence in the last year**
- **93,500 babies under 1 year old live with a parent who is a problem drinker**
- **144,000 babies under 1 year old live with a parent who has a common mental health problem**
- **In both England and Wales, neglect is the most common category of abuse for under-1s subject to a child protection plan, followed by emotional abuse, physical abuse, multiple abuse and sexual abuse**

All Babies Count: Prevention and protection for vulnerable babies
Credit: NSPCC report by Chris Cuthbert, Gwynne Rayns and Kate Stanley (2011)

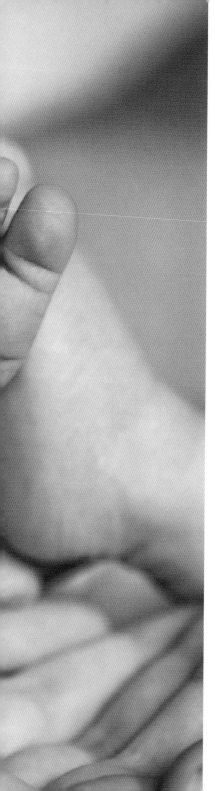

VULNERABILITY OF DISABLED CHILDREN

Disabled children have an equal right to protection, yet barriers can exist at all stages of the child protection process.

Factors that increase risk and lessen protection include:

- Attitudes and assumptions that do not treat disabled children equally and have an impact on all aspects of their lives
- Reluctance to believe disabled children are abused, minimising the impact of abuse and mistakenly attributing indicators of abuse to a child's impairment
- Barriers to the provision of support services that lead to the disabled child and their family being isolated
- Impairment-related factors such as dependency on a number of carers for personal assistance, impaired capacity to resist or avoid abuse, communication impairments and an inability to understand what is happening or to seek help
- Barriers to communication and seeking help where the child's opportunities for seeking help may be very limited

Disabled children at greatest risk of abuse are those with behaviour disorders. Other high-risk groups include children with learning difficulties/disabilities, children with speech and language difficulties, children with health-related conditions and deaf children.

Evidence on risk and severity of impairment is mixed. Most research suggests that disabled boys are at greater risk of abuse than disabled girls when compared to non-disabled children.

There is a lack of knowledge about the differing risks to disabled children at the various stages of their development although there is some evidence that for maltreated children with health and communication impairments, there is a greater number of first incidents of maltreatment from birth to five years of age. Disabled children in residential care face particular risks.

VULNERABILITY OF DISABLED CHILDREN – WHAT RESEARCH SUGGESTS *

Disabled children are more likely to be abused by someone in their family compared to non-disabled children. The majority of disabled children are abused by someone who is known to them.

Research also suggests that significant numbers of children with harmful sexual behaviour have learning difficulties or disabilities, although caution should be exercised in interpreting these findings.

Bullying is a feature in the lives of many disabled children.

Research indicates that disabled children are more likely to experience the negative aspects of social networking sites than non-disabled children.

Disabled children (and severely disabled children even more so) may disclose less frequently and delay disclosure more often compared to typically developing children. Disabled children are most likely to turn to a trusted adult they know well for help such as family, friend or teacher.

> *
> 'We have the right to be safe'
> Protecting disabled children from abuse.
> NSPCC October 2014

WHAT IS A CHILD OR ADULT IN NEED?

A child or adult in need are people who are unlikely to reach or maintain a satisfactory level of health or development, or their health and development will be significantly impaired, without the provision of services, plus those who are disabled.

This can also include children who are themselves young carers who may need support.

It is sometimes easy to jump to conclusions about a person's upbringing or welfare if it appears different to our own.

We should be careful not to make assumptions but to remain aware of the five themes in 'every child matters', the possible signs and indicators of abuse and to maintain a child rather than an adult focus.

Concerns about a person's welfare and safety are on a continuum. In most cases, it is not possible to know how serious cases are without an assessment being carried out. The legal framework sets out the duties, powers and circumstances under which the local authority can and must become involved when there are concerns about a child's welfare or safety.

Children are raised in different ways and patterns of family life vary. There is no one perfect way to raise a child.

Routine, meeting basic needs, setting behavioural boundaries and discipline, keeping the child safe, loved and appropriately clothed, can appear differently in every culture.

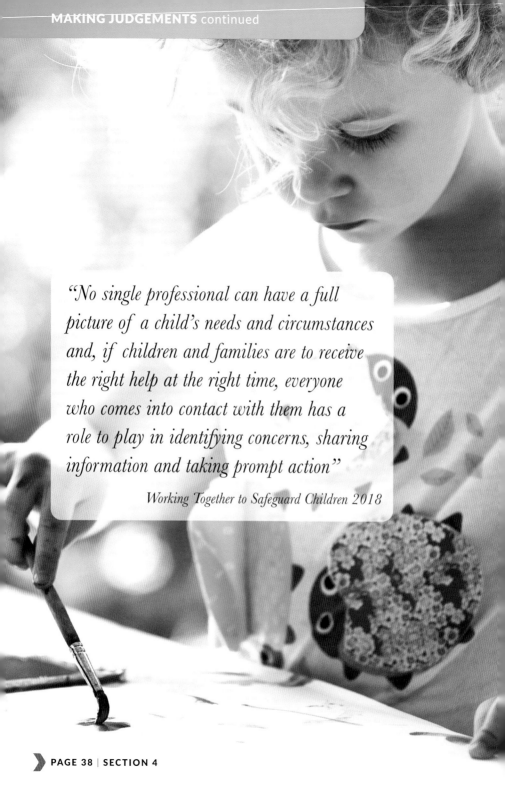

"*No single professional can have a full picture of a child's needs and circumstances and, if children and families are to receive the right help at the right time, everyone who comes into contact with them has a role to play in identifying concerns, sharing information and taking prompt action*"

Working Together to Safeguard Children 2018

EVERY CHILD MATTERS: THE FIVE OUTCOMES

When the government developed the 'every child matters' initiative, children, young people and their families were consulted on what they wanted the government to achieve.

The five outcomes which mattered the most were:

1. ACHIEVE ECONOMIC WELL-BEING

Parents, carers and families are encouraged to be economically active:

- **Engage in further education, employment or training on leaving school**
- **Ready for employment**
- **Live in decent homes and sustainable communities**
- **Access to transport and material goods**
- **Live in households free from low income**

BE HEALTHY

Parents, carers and families to promote healthy choices:

- **Physically healthy**
- **Mentally and emotionally healthy**
- **Sexually healthy**
- **Healthy lifestyles**
- **Choose not to take illegal drugs**

3. STAY SAFE

Parents, carers and families to provide safe homes and stability:

- Safe from maltreatment, neglect, violence and sexual exploitation
- Safe from accidental injury and death
- Safe from bullying and discrimination
- Safe from crime and anti-social behaviour in and out of school
- Have security, stability and are cared for

4. ENJOY AND ACHIEVE

Parents, carers and families to support learning:

- Ready for school
- Attend and enjoy school
- Achieve stretching national educational standards at primary school
- Achieve personal and social development and enjoy recreation
- Achieve stretching national educational standards at secondary school

5. MAKE A POSITIVE CONTRIBUTION

Parents, carers and families to promote positive behaviour:

- Engage in decision making and support in the community and environment
- Engage in law abiding and positive behaviour in and out of school
- Develop positive relationships and choose not to bully or discriminate
- Develop self-confidence and successfully deal with significant live changes and challenges
- Develop enterprising behaviour

CHILDREN'S VIEWS *

Some of the views of children are publicised in the current 'Working together to safeguard children' guidance document.

Children have said that they need:

- **Vigilance:** To have adults notice when things are troubling them
- **Understanding and action:** To understand what is happening; to be heard and understood; and to have that understanding acted upon
- **Stability:** To be able to develop an on-going stable relationship of trust with those helping them
- **Respect:** To be treated with the expectation that they are competent rather than not
- **Information and engagement:** To be informed about and involved in procedures, decisions, concerns and plans
- **Explanation:** To be informed of the outcome of assessments and decisions and reasons when their views have not been met with a positive response
- **Support:** To be provided with support in their own right as well as a member of their family
- **Advocacy:** To be provided with support to assist them in putting forward their views

HM Government, Working together to safeguard children
2018

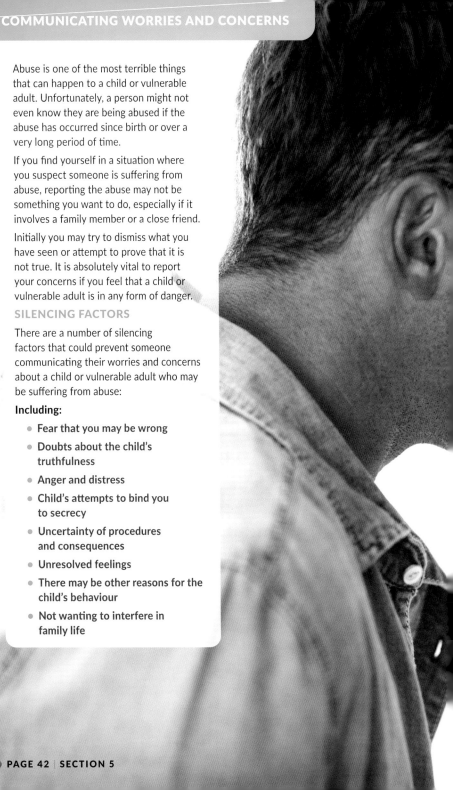

Abuse is one of the most terrible things that can happen to a child or vulnerable adult. Unfortunately, a person might not even know they are being abused if the abuse has occurred since birth or over a very long period of time.

If you find yourself in a situation where you suspect someone is suffering from abuse, reporting the abuse may not be something you want to do, especially if it involves a family member or a close friend.

Initially you may try to dismiss what you have seen or attempt to prove that it is not true. It is absolutely vital to report your concerns if you feel that a child or vulnerable adult is in any form of danger.

SILENCING FACTORS

There are a number of silencing factors that could prevent someone communicating their worries and concerns about a child or vulnerable adult who may be suffering from abuse:

Including:

- **Fear that you may be wrong**
- **Doubts about the child's truthfulness**
- **Anger and distress**
- **Child's attempts to bind you to secrecy**
- **Uncertainty of procedures and consequences**
- **Unresolved feelings**
- **There may be other reasons for the child's behaviour**
- **Not wanting to interfere in family life**

WHO ARE CHILDREN LIKELY TO TURN TO?

- Friends
- Mothers
- Fathers
- Other trusted adult

The majority of children and young people identify at least one person they can talk to. Unfortunately, a significant minority of children do not feel they have anyone they can trust to share their worries with.

THE FOUR MAIN CHARACTERISTICS OF AN ADULT THAT CHILDREN CAN TRUST

1. **Being there:** Children and young people having the general feeling that an adult is there for them
2. **Proving themselves:** taking the time to Listen, acting appropriately and keeping promises
3. **Having the right attitude:** not losing their temper or trying to take over
4. **Knowing what they're talking about:** Sharing relevant experience and not acting as if they know more than they do

CONCERNS ABOUT A CHILD'S OR VULNERABLE ADULT'S WELFARE CAN COME TO LIGHT IN MANY WAYS, INCLUDING:

- Disclosure from a child, parent or anonymously
- Letter, phone call or email
- Appearance of a child: Inappropriate, dirty, ill-fitting clothing
- Behaviour of a child: Emulating adult behaviour
- Behaviour of a parent toward the child: Aggressive or violent
- An observation made of an abusive incident
- Report of bullying
- Witnessing domestic abuse where children are in the home
- Being informed of a concern by a work colleague
- Self-harm or reckless conduct of a pregnant mother
- Self-disclosure of an adult
- Material evidence found or provided
- Whistleblowing by staff about a staff member

SAFEGUARDING IS EVERYONE'S BUSINESS ...

Everyone who works with, or comes into contact with children or vulnerable adults, have a part to play in safeguarding and promoting the individuals' welfare.

SAFEGUARDING PARTNERS

Government agencies have a significant involvement in safeguarding and promoting the welfare of individuals. This is led by three key bodies who make up the local safeguarding partnership:

- **Local authorities**
- **Chief officers of police**
- **Clinical commissioning groups (Health)**

The key responsibilities of the safeguarding partnership are to:

- **Involve relevant agencies in the area**
- **Identify and supervise the review of serious safeguarding cases**
- **Publish local safeguarding arrangements**
- **Arrange for independent scrutiny of their arrangements**
- **To publish annual review report on their safeguarding activities**

AGENCY INVOLVEMENT

The Children Act 1989 enables local authorities to request help from the agencies and places a responsibility on those agencies to co-operate with children's social care services in safeguarding and promoting the welfare of children.

Children's social care services are also required to give due regard to a child's wishes when determining what services to provide under section 17 of the Children Act 1989 and before making decisions about action to be taken to protect individual children under section 47 of the Children Act 1989.

Other agencies and individuals involved in safeguarding children and vulnerable adults have a responsibility to pass on to the local authority or the police any concerns about a child. These agencies also have a duty to work with the local safeguarding partnership when required.

These include:

- **Education, including independent settings**
- **The probation and rehabilitation teams**
- **The fire service**
- **Community, sports, faith and charity groups**

ROLES AND RESPONSIBILITIES OF THE SAFEGUARDING LEAD

The safeguarding lead would ideally be a person who has:

- An interest in making a difference in the organisation
- A good basic knowledge of safeguarding and child protection
- The ability to be child centric
- The support of management to undertake the role
- Status and authority to make decisions and professional judgements
- Excellent rapport with children, families and staff
- Ability to communicate to a high standard, both verbally and in writing

Some of the key responsibilities include:

- Being the central point of contact in an organisation for safeguarding children and adults
- Responding to any safeguarding concerns within the organisation
- To seek support and advice from other professionals
- Recognising signs and indicators of abuse and neglect
- Keeping records safe and compliant in line with the Data Protection Act
- Promoting welfare and safeguarding related policies and procedures

NOTE:

It is not the safeguarding lead's responsibility to investigate or assess whether a child in their care is suffering or likely to suffer significant harm. This is the role of Children's Social Care Services within the local authorities.

The safeguarding lead has also historically been referred to, within an organisation, as the:

- **Nominated Welfare Officer (NWO)**
- **Lead Welfare Officer (LWO)**
- **Senior Designated Professional (SDP)**

MASH (MULTI-AGENCY SAFEGUARDING HUB)

Several high-profile safeguarding cases have highlighted the tragic consequences which can result when information indicating risk is held by one agency and not appropriately shared with others.

In light of this, many areas have established Multi-Agency Safeguarding Hubs to reduce the chances of cases slipping through the system.

The Multi-Agency Safeguarding Hub (MASH) brings key professionals together to facilitate early, better quality information sharing, analysis and decision-making, to safeguard more effectively.

Multi-Agency Safeguarding Hubs are supported by the local safeguarding partnerships and social care services and co-locate local authorities, the police and health services, enabling real time information sharing, decision making and communication.

The benefits of MASH:

- **More accurate assessment of risk and need**
- **More thorough and driven management of cases**
- **Better understanding between professions**
- **Greater efficiencies in processes and resources**

LOCAL AUTHORITY DESIGNATED OFFICER (LADO)

Every local authority has a statutory duty to employ a Local Authority Designated Officer (LADO). The LADO is employed within children's social care services with the specific role to examine allegations made against volunteers or staff who work with children.

The Local Authority Designated Officer is responsible for:

- **Providing information, advice and guidance**
- **Managing and overseeing individual cases**
- **Monitoring progress of cases to ensure they are managed efficiently**
- **Liaising with the police and other key agencies**

CARE QUALITY COMMISSION (CQC)

The independent regulators of health and social care in England.

The CQC are responsible for inspecting all registered health services provided to children and work in partnership with other inspectorates.

Children's social care services are regulated by the Care Quality Commission.

SAFEGUARDING POLICY

A safeguarding policy is a statement defining what the organisation will do to ensure the safety of children and/or vulnerable adults.

Safeguarding policies can include:

- **Aims and objectives**
- **Definitions**
- **The legal framework that supports the policy**
- **Organisational responsibilities**
- **Arrangements for implementation** (what the organisation will do to meet their targets and objectives)
- **Other workplace policies that relate to safeguarding**
- **Equality statement**
- **Staff training requirements**
- **Review dates and authorising signatories**

Other workplace policies that relate to safeguarding include:

- **Whistle blowing**
- **Recruitment**
- **Complaints**
- **Health and safety**
- **Procedures for dealing with allegations of abuse including allegations made against other children**
- **Bullying and harassment**
- **Photography and filming**
- **Equality**
- **E-Safety**

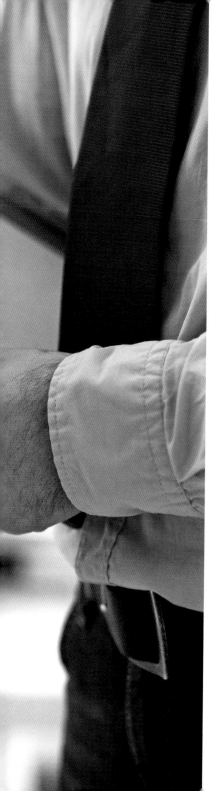

SOCIAL CARE SERVICES

Local authority social care services support families and safeguard children, young people and vulnerable adults who may be at risk of abuse or neglect.

Social care encompasses many areas of need, each with a level of specialist services.

Children, young people and families

This includes preventative family support and child protection services, child placement, fostering, adoption, working with young offenders, children and young people who have learning or physical disabilities as well as support for families and carers.

Vulnerable adults

This includes support for the elderly, people with mental health problems, learning or physical disabilities, those with alcohol and substance misuse problems, the homeless, prevention of abuse or neglect, domestic abuse and associated support for families and carers.

MAKING A REFERRAL

Referrals can be made by any member of the public, or by other professionals who are working with the child, vulnerable adult or their families.

Professionals in all agencies who come into contact with children, who work with adult parents/carers or who gain knowledge about children through working with adults should:

- **Be alert to potential indicators of abuse or neglect**
- **Be alert to the risks which individual abusers or potential abusers may pose to children**
- **Be alert to the impact on the child of any concerns of abuse or maltreatment**
- **Be able to gather and analyse information as part of an assessment of the child's needs**

If people in organisations do not feel competent to make the referral personally, the designated safeguarding lead should be notified who will then make contact with the local social care services, the police or the NSPCC about the concerns raised and to complete the appropriate referral form using the information gathered.

The information will include:

- **Individual's name, date of birth and address**
- **Parents/carers name and contact details**
- **Name of GP**
- **Ethnicity and religion if known**
- **What has been recognised or recognised to prompt the referral**
- **What actions have been taken to date**
- **Your contact details**

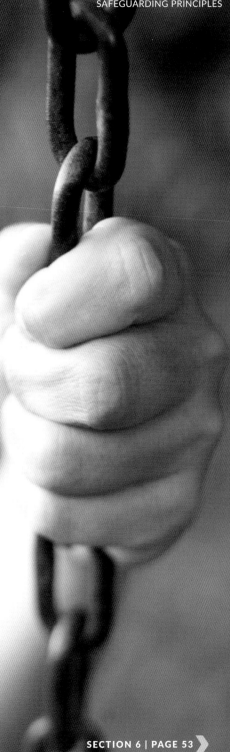

SOCIAL CARE SERVICES ARE EXPECTED TO:

- Discuss your concerns
- Decide what action is needed
- Agree with you what the child and parents are told, by whom and when
- Involve the police if a crime may have been committed
- Tell you if they are taking no further action and why
- Acknowledge your written referral within one working day of receipt
- Check if the child is the subject of a child protection plan
- Consult with other agencies
- Take action to ensure the child is safe

If social care services decide the child is at risk of immediate and significant harm, prompt emergency action will be taken. This is likely to involve a section 47 enquiry.

SECTION 47 ENQUIRY

Section 47 of the Children Act 1989 places a duty on local authorities to investigate and make enquiries into referrals and the circumstances of children considered to be at risk of 'significant harm' and, where these enquiries indicate the need, to decide what action, if any, it may need to take to safeguard and promote the child's welfare.

The child's welfare must remain paramount in the minds of those undertaking the investigation and consideration of the child's short and long term best interests will govern all decisions and actions.

Everyone has a duty to share information regarding concerns they may have about the welfare of a child or vulnerable adult.

Where there are concerns about the safety of a child or vulnerable adult, the sharing of information in a timely and effective manner between organisations is very important and can reduce the risk of harm.

No individual should assume that someone else will pass on information which they think may be critical to keeping someone safe.

Fears about sharing information cannot stand in the way of the need to promote the welfare and protect the safety of that person. However, confidentiality should be maintained at all times. Information should be handled and shared with relevant others on a need to know basis only.

Concerns should only be shared privately and formally with relevant people and should not be discussed:

- **With other parents or carers**
- **Outside of work with family and friends**

This would be seen as a breach of confidentiality and could be a disciplinary matter. The sharing of information with other relevant people should only be with a view to best safeguard the person and should be within 24 hours of the initial concern.

You should never agree to keeping secrets with a child or vulnerable adult and should always let them know that you may have to share what they are telling you with others, but only with others who will help to protect them and keep them safe.

You learn about how concerns may be raised through:

- **Behaviours**
- **Appearances**
- **Relationships with their parents, carers or significant others**

Concerns may also be raised about a child or vulnerable adult by a:

- **Parent**
- **Sibling**
- **Colleague**
- **Neighbour**
- **Member of the public**
- **Another child or adult at risk**
- **An anonymous person, by phone, e-mail or face to face with no name given**
- **Above all by the individual themselves**

It is good practice to share the concerns raised with the child's family, except in circumstances where the safety of the child or others is further compromised or evidence relating to a potential crime could be removed or contaminated.

DECIDING TO SHARE INFORMATION

A useful publication to help you make decisions about sharing personal information on a case by case basis is:

Information Sharing: *Advice for practitioners providing safeguarding services to children, young people, parents and carers (July 2018)*

This advice helps practitioners and senior managers decide when and how to share personal information legally and professionally. It might also be helpful for practitioners working with adults who are responsible for children who may be in need.

This replaces 'Information Sharing: Advice for practitioners providing safeguarding services (2015)'.

WHEN AND HOW TO SHARE INFORMATION

When asked to share information, you should consider the following questions to help you decide if and when to share. If the decision is taken to share, you should consider how best to effectively share the information.

WHEN

Is there a clear and legitimate purpose for sharing information?

- **Yes – see next question**
- **No – do not share**

Does the information enable an individual to be identified?

- **Yes – see next question**
- **No – you can share but should consider how**

Is the information confidential?

- **Yes – see next question**
- **No – you can share but should consider how**

Do you have consent?

- **Yes – you can share but should consider how**
- **No – see next question**

Is there another reason to share information such as to fulfil a public function or to protect the vital interests of the information subject?

- **Yes – you can share but should consider how**
- **No – do not share**

HOW

- **Identify how much information to share**
- **Distinguish fact from opinion**
- **Ensure that you are giving the right information to the right individual**
- **Ensure where possible that you are sharing the information securely**
- **Inform the individual that the information has been shared if they were not aware of this, as long as this would not create or increase risk of harm**

* All information sharing decisions and reasons must be recorded in line with your organisation or local procedures. If at any stage you are unsure about how or when to share information, you should seek advice and ensure that the outcome of the discussion is recorded. If there are concerns that a person is suffering or likely to suffer significant harm, then follow the relevant procedures without delay

Information sharing: Advice for practitioners providing safeguarding services to
children, young people, parents and carers (July 2018)

THE SEVEN GOLDEN RULES TO SHARING INFORMATION

1. Remember the Data Protection Act 2018 is not a barrier to sharing information
2. Be open and honest
3. Seek advice
4. Share with consent where appropriate
5. Consider safety and well-being
6. Necessary, proportionate, relevant, accurate, timely and secure
7. Keep a record

HM Government, Information Sharing: *Advice for practitioners providing safeguarding services to children, young people, parents and carers (July 2018)*

Golden rules

It can be hard to conceive that abuse does exist or that anyone can deliberately harm a child or someone who is vulnerable.

It is without doubt an emotive subject and where we become aware of abuse and are involved in necessary processes to best safeguard a person we may need to seek professional support in order to deal with our responses.

A child may have talked to several people about an issue of abuse before they talked to you or it may be the first time they have told their story.

FACTORS PREVENTING DISCLOSURE

The key barriers preventing children and vulnerable adults from communicating their concerns can include:

- **Having no one to turn to regarding their concerns**
- **Not wanting to burden others**
- **Fears and anxieties manipulated by the perpetrator**
- **Developmental barriers**
- **Emotional barriers**
- **Anxiety over the confidentiality of the information they provide**

DISCLOSURE OF ABUSE CAN OCCUR THROUGH A VARIETY OF MEANS:

- **Verbally**
- **Appearance**
- **Behaviour**
- **Role play or re-enacting**
- **Drawing pictures**
- **Writing stories**

RESPONDING TO DISCLOSURE

If you are approached by a child, young person or vulnerable adult with a disclosure that they are being, or have been abused;

- **Stay calm and collective**
- **Listen very carefully to what is being said to you and do not interrupt**
- **Always reassure the individual and be sympathetic**
- **Do not make jokes or change the subject**
- **Do not make disbelieving comments for example;**

    "He would never do that to you surely" or

    "I'm sure they didn't mean it"

- **Tell the individual that they have done the right thing in telling you and you are treating the information seriously**

- **Record the information, including a written note of the observation, the date and time and the person's present**
- **Explain to the individual that you will need to communicate their concerns with the appropriate person, such as the safeguarding lead or line manager**
- **Report to the safeguarding lead or line manager with the information you have gathered**

Do not:

- Make promises
- Promise to keep secrets
- Be judgmental
- Make contact with the alleged abuser
- Pass on the information to anyone other than those who are designated to manage disclosures
- Pressurise the individual to disclose further details
- Stop the individual when they are telling you what has happened to them, as they may never tell you again

RECORDING INFORMATION

It is vital that information is recorded and a detailed report is produced at the time of disclosure.

This may include:

- Details of the individuals involved including the victim and the alleged perpetrator (if disclosed), including names, address details, date of birth, ethnic origin and any disabilities they may have
- Information regarding the nature of the allegation
- A description of any incident or injury sustained
- Time, date, location and any persons' present
- A concise account of what is said by the victim, using their own words
- Information about any action to be taken by you or others
- Details of the person recording the information (name, role, contact details)
- Keep a record of any third-party correspondence (e.g. police officer, social care services etc.)

REFERRAL INFORMATION

All referral information and decisions, phone calls, discussions and actions should be recorded and kept with the full record of disclosure.

This should also include a record of any decisions made not to refer the incident, along with the reasons.

You may use any type of paper or incident form for your recordings but try not to use personal diaries and notebooks, as they could become evidence in the future.

If an individual is at imminent risk you must not delay. Obtain urgent medical treatment if required and contact social care services immediately, or the police in an emergency.

Adults and even children may also disclose that they have abused, or do abuse children and/or vulnerable adults. All such disclosures must be taken seriously and dealt with in the same way as previously described.

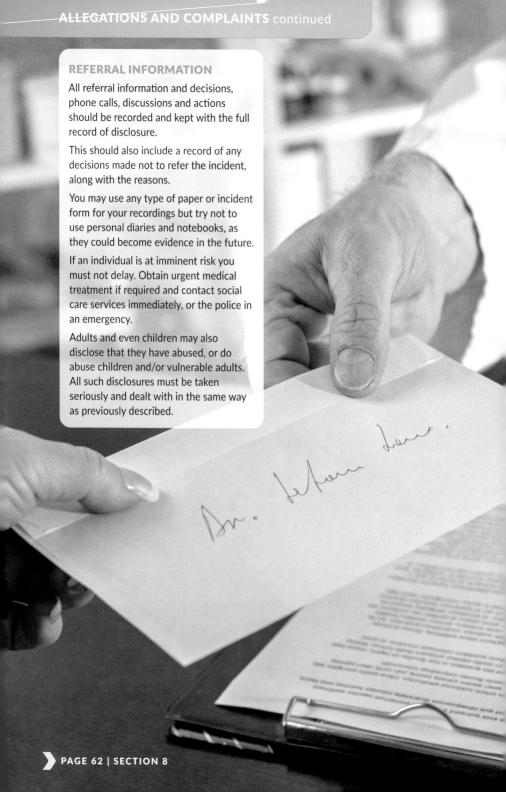

ALLEGATIONS AND COMPLAINTS IN THE WORKPLACE

In any situation where concerns are raised or allegations are made about another member of staff or even yourself, you must report them immediately to either the safeguarding lead or the designated manager.

If the concerns or allegations are about one of the persons you need to report to, you should report to the one which is not involved, or seek advice from social care services.

You must not discuss the concerns or allegations directly with the staff members concerned.

There should be procedures within all organisations who come into contact with children and/or vulnerable adults, to deal with any concerns or allegations made against staff.

SAFEGUARDING FAILINGS

Much of today's safeguarding law and practices have sadly been informed by serious case reviews that have taken place after the death of a child or vulnerable adult.

Around 80 children die each year as a result of abuse or neglect and the review of each death shows that the child's vulnerabilities were complex.

Some of the failings to prevent these deaths have been:

- **Poor communication**
- **Failure to share information and work together across agencies**
- **Lack of procedural direction**
- **Poor inter-agency working**
- **Lack of awareness of signs of abuse**
- **Focusing on the adults and not being child centred**

High standards of professional practice and confidence in safeguarding policies and procedures are part of a good preventative strategy to avoid complaints. Complaints can appear trivial where others are of a more serious nature. They should all be given fair and equal attention.

Families experiencing safeguarding or child protection processes may be under a significant amount of stress. Even though they may have been responsible for the potential abuse or neglect of a child, they still have a right to complain about issues they are unhappy with.

These complaints can only be in regard to the process and not the issues related to the lead up to and details of the allegations of abuse. These matters will be considered within the organisation's safeguarding policy.

Safeguarding Leads' can reduce the risks of complaints and allegations by:

- Having safe systems of work in place
- Having clear, documented policies and procedures which are made available to all staff members, as well as parents and carers
- Maintaining accurate and up-to-date records for each child
- Ensuring all staff and volunteers are aged 16 years or over and have received a Disclosure and Barring Service (DBS) check
- Documenting any marks or injuries which children may have when they arrive and requesting parents/carers to sign the record
- Making sure children are supervised at all times
- Nurturing positive, open and honest communications with children, vulnerable adults, parents and carers
- Reporting all allegations to the Local Authority Designated Officer (LADO) without delay
- Liaising with the police if a criminal investigation takes place
- Be willing to talk with the child and family and explain the actions taken
- Advise the senior management of possible disciplinary action
- Share only essential information with the worker, LADO and senior management

PROTECTING YOURSELF AGAINST ALLEGATIONS AND COMPLAINTS

The majority of adults who work with children or vulnerable adults act professionally and aim to provide a safe and supportive environment which secures the well-being and very best outcomes for the people in their care.

However, it is recognised that in this area of work tensions and misunderstandings can occur. It is here that the behaviour of adults can give rise to allegations of abuse being made against them.

Equally, some allegations reported will be genuine and there are people who will deliberately seek out, create or exploit opportunities to abuse others. It is therefore essential that all possible steps are taken to safeguard children and vulnerable adults, and ensure that the adults working with them are safe to do so.

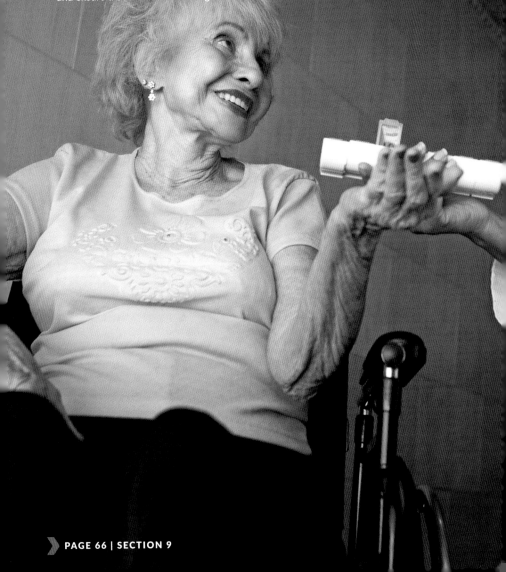

KEEPING YOURSELF SAFE

It is important that everyone working in a position of trust considers safer working practice that helps to keep themselves, vulnerable adults and children safe.

It is helpful to be aware of situations that may make staff feel more vulnerable or could be open to misunderstanding, for example, where the individual needs to be provided with personal care or where staff are working alone.

WHAT HELPS?

- Guidelines to support safer working practice so that everyone has a clear understanding of how these areas are managed and protocols in the setting

- Always think about how your actions could be interpreted and tell your SDP or manager if anything makes you feel uncomfortable

- Having a culture in the workplace where you are able to ask for support and discuss best practice

- Good recording practice in relation to any incidents of concern

- Keep your personal details separate from your professional role and consider how you use social media and what privacy settings you have in place

- E-Safety policies help to promote safe use of technology together with acceptable use agreements and permissions for photography

PROPRIETY AND BEHAVIOUR

DO NOT:

- Use oppressive language
- Engage in sexual activity under 18 years
- Be alone away from others
- Engage in horseplay
- Use inappropriate touching
- Encourage children to use inappropriate language
- Provide personal care
- Store photos on a mobile phone or share photos on social media
- Behave in a manner which would lead any reasonable person to question their suitability to work with children or act as a role model

DO:

- Promote fairness
- Confront and deal with bullying
- Be a role model
- Train in open environments
- Maintain a safe and appropriate relationship
- Avoid unnecessary physical contact
- Communicate with parents regularly
- Keep up-to-date
- Be aware that behaviour in your personal lives may impact upon your work with children
- Follow any codes of conduct deemed appropriate by your work

DUTY OF CARE

- Understand the responsibilities, which are part of your employment or role and be aware that sanctions will be applied if these provisions are breached

- Always act and be seen to act, in the individual's best interests

- Avoid any conduct which would lead any reasonable person to question your motivation and intentions

- Take responsibility for your own actions and behaviour

- Foster a culture of openness and support

- Ensure that systems are in place for concerns to be raised

- Ensure that there is in place effective recording systems which confirm discussions, decisions and the outcomes of any actions taken

- Ensure that staff are not placed in situations which render them particularly vulnerable

- Ensure that all staff are aware of expectations, policies and procedures

INFATUATIONS

- Report and record any incidents or indications (verbal, written or physical) that suggest a child or young person may have developed an infatuation with a member of staff

- Always acknowledge and maintain professional boundaries

CONFIDENTIALITY

- Be clear about when information can be shared and in what circumstances it is appropriate to do so
- Treat information received about children or vulnerable adults in a discreet and confidential manner
- Seek advice from a senior member of staff if in any doubt about sharing information
- Be aware of whom any concerns or allegations should be reported to

DRESS AND APPEARANCE

Adults should wear clothing which:

- Is appropriate to their role
- Is not likely to be viewed as offensive, revealing or sexually provocative
- Does not distract, cause embarrassment or give rise to misunderstanding
- Is absent of any political or otherwise contentious slogans
- Is not considered to be discriminatory and is culturally sensitive

USE OF PERSONAL LIVING SPACE

Adults should:

- Be vigilant in maintaining their privacy and mindful of the need to avoid placing themselves in vulnerable situations
- Challenge any request for their accommodation to be used as an additional resource for the workplace
- Be mindful of the need to maintain professional boundaries
- Refrain from asking children or adults to undertake personal jobs or errands

COMMUNICATION

Adults should:

- Ensure that personal social networking sites are set at private and children are never listed as approved contacts
- Not give their personal contact details to children, including their mobile telephone number
- Only use equipment e.g. Mobile phones, provided by work to communicate with children, making sure that parents have given permission for this form of communication to be used
- Only make contact with children for professional reasons and in accordance with any school or work policy
- Recognise that text messaging should only be used as part of an agreed protocol and when other forms of communication are not possible
- Not use the internet or web-based communication channels to send personal messages to a child or young person

SEXUAL CONTACT

Adults should not:

- Have sexual relationships with children
- Have any form of communication with a child or young person which could be interpreted as sexually suggestive or provocative i.e. verbal comments, letters, notes, electronic mail, phone calls, texts and physical contact
- Make sexual remarks to, or about, a child or young person
- Discuss their own sexual relationships with, or in the presence of children

Adults should:

- Ensure that their relationships with children clearly take place within the boundaries of a respectful professional relationship
- Take care that their language or conduct does not give rise to comment or speculation. Attitudes, demeanour and language all require care and thought, particularly when members of staff are dealing with adolescent boys and girls

PHYSICAL CONTACT

Adults should:

- Be aware that even well intentioned physical contact may be misconstrued by the child, an observer or by anyone to whom this action is described

- Never touch a child in a way which may be considered indecent

- Always be prepared to report and explain actions and accept that all physical contact be open to scrutiny

- Always encourage children, where possible, to undertake self-care tasks independently

- Work within health and safety regulations

- Be aware of cultural or religious views about touching and always be sensitive to issues of gender

- Understand that physical contact in some circumstances can be easily misinterpreted

CHILDREN AND YOUNG PEOPLE IN DISTRESS

Adults should:

- Consider the way in which they offer comfort and reassurance to a distressed child and do it in an age appropriate way
- Be cautious in offering reassurance in one to one situations, but always record such actions in these circumstances
- Follow professional guidance or code of practice
- Record and report situations which may give rise to concern from either party
- Not assume that all children seek physical comfort if they are distressed

PERSONAL CARE

Young people are entitled to respect and privacy at all times and especially when in a state of undress, changing clothes, bathing or undertaking any form of personal care. There are occasions where there will be a need for an appropriate level of supervision in order to safeguard young people and to satisfy health and safety considerations. This supervision should be appropriate to the needs and age of the young people concerned and sensitive to the potential for embarrassment. Adults need to be vigilant about their own behaviour, ensure they follow agreed guidelines and be mindful of the needs of the children with whom they work.

This means that adults should:

- **Avoid any physical contact when children are in a state of undress**
- **Avoid any visually intrusive behaviour**
- **Where there are changing rooms, announce your intention of entering**

This means that adults should not:

- **Change in the same place as children**
- **Shower or bathe with children**
- **Assist with any personal care task which a child or young person can undertake by themselves**

FIRST AID AND THE ADMINISTRATION OF MEDICATION

Health and safety legislation places duties on all employers to ensure appropriate health and safety polices and equipment are in place and an appropriate person is appointed to take charge of First Aid arrangements.

Some children may need medication during school hours. In circumstances where children need medication regularly, a health care plan should be drawn up to ensure the safety and protection of children and staff.

With the permission of parents, children should be encouraged to self-administer medication or treatment including, for example any ointment, sun cream or the use of inhalers.

If a member of staff is concerned or uncertain about the amount or type of medication being given to a child, this should be discussed with the appropriate senior colleague at the earliest opportunity. When administering first aid, wherever possible, staff should ensure that another adult is present, or aware of the action that is being taken.

Parents and carers should always be informed when first aid has been administered.

Adults should:

- Adhere to policies for administering first aid or medication
- Comply with the necessary reporting requirements
- Make other adults aware of the task being undertaken
- Explain to the child what is happening
- Always act and be seen to act in the child's best interests
- Report and record any administration of first aid or medication
- Have regard to any health plan which is in place
- Always ensure that an appropriate risk assessment is undertaken prior to undertaking certain activities

ONE TO ONE SITUATIONS

Every organisation working with or on behalf of children should consider one to one situations when drawing up their policies.

It is not realistic to state that one to one situations should never take place. It is however, appropriate to state that where there is a need, agreed with a senior manager and the parents or carers, for an adult to be alone with a child or young person, certain procedures and clear safeguards must be in place.

One to one situations have the potential to make a child more vulnerable to harm by those who seek to exploit their position of trust. Adults working in one to one settings with children may also be more vulnerable to unjust or unfounded allegations being made against them. Both possibilities should be recognised so that when one to one situations are unavoidable, reasonable and sensible precautions are taken.

PHOTOGRAPHY AND VIDEOS

Working with children may involve the taking or recording of images. Any such work should take place with due regard to the law and the need to safeguard the privacy, dignity, safety and well-being of children. Informed written consent from parents or carers and agreement, where possible, from the child or young person, should always be sought before an image is taken for any purpose.

Careful consideration should be given as to how activities involving the taking of images are organised and undertaken. Care should be taken to ensure that all parties understand the implications of the image being taken especially if it is to be used for any publicity purposes or published in the media, or on the internet.

It is not appropriate for adults to take photographs of children for their personal use. It is recommended that when using a photograph the following guidance should be followed:

- **If the photograph is used, avoid naming the child**
- **If the child is named, avoid using their photograph**
- **Schools should establish whether the image will be retained for further use**
- **Images should be securely stored and used only by those authorised to do so**

The Victoria Climbié Inquiry: report of an inquiry by Lord Laming 28th January 2003
www.gov.uk/government/publications/the-victoria-climbie-inquiry-report-of-an-inquiry-by-lord-laming

Statement of Government Policy on Adult Safeguarding Department of Health, 2013
www.gov.uk/government/publications/adult-safeguarding-statement-of-government-policy-10-may-2013

Every child matters
www.gov.uk/government/publications/every-child-matters

Working Together to Safeguard Children (2018)
www.gov.uk/government/publications/working-together-to-safeguard-children

What to do if you're worried a child is being abused (2015)
www.gov.uk/government/publications/what-to-do-if-youre-worried-a-child-is-being-abused--2

Keeping children safe in education (2021)
www.gov.uk/government/publications/keeping-children-safe-in-education--2

The United Nations Convention on the Rights of the Child 1989
www.unicef.org.uk/what-we-do/un-convention-child-rights

Mental Capacity Act - Code of Practice
www.gov.uk/government/publications/mental-capacity-act-code-of-practice

Prevent strategy
www.gov.uk/government/publications/prevent-strategy-2011

Channel guidance
www.gov.uk/government/publications/channel-guidance

Information Sharing: Advice for practitioners providing safeguarding services to children, young people, parents and carers (2018)
www.gov.uk/government/publications/safeguarding-practitioners-information-sharing-advice

NSPCC report: All Babies Count: prevention and protection for vulnerable babies
Authors: Chris Cuthbert, Gwynne Rayns and Kate Stanley
www.nspcc.org.uk/services-and-resources/research-and-resources/pre-2013/all-babies-count/

NSPCC report: 'We have the right to be safe' Protecting disabled children from abuse
Authors: David Miller and Jon Brown
www.nspcc.org.uk/services-and-resources/research-and-resources/2014/right-to-be-safe/